Kwanzaa

Rebecca Rissman

Heinemann Library
Chicago, Illinois

www.heinemannraintree.com

Visit our website to find out more information about Heinemann-Raintree books.

To order:

☎ Phone 888-454-2279

💻 Visit www.heinemannraintree.com to browse our catalog and order online.

©2011 Heinemann Library
an imprint of Capstone Global Library, LLC
Chicago, Illinois

Edited by Adrian Vigliano and Rebecca Rissman
Designed by Ryan Frieson
Picture research by Tracy Cummins
Leveling by Nancy E. Harris
Originated by Capstone Global Library Ltd.
Printed and bound in the United States of America, North Mankato, MN

15 14 13 12
10 9 8 7 6 5 4 3 2

Library of Congress Cataloging-in-Publication Data
Rissman, Rebecca.
 Kwanzaa / Rebecca Rissman.
     p. cm.—(Holidays and festivals)
 Includes bibliographical references and index.
 ISBN 978-1-4329-4061-4 (hc)—ISBN 978-1-4329-4080-5 (pb) 1.
Kwanzaa—Juvenile literature. 2. African Americans—Social life and
customs—Juvenile literature. I. Title.
 GT4403.R58 2011
 394.2612—dc22
2009052871

052012
006721RP

Acknowledgments

The author and publishers are grateful to the following for permission to reproduce copyright material: Corbis ©Strauss/Curtis **p.4**; Corbis ©Rolf Bruderer **p.6**; Corbis ©Aristide Economopoulos/Star Ledger **pp.7**, **17**; Corbis ©Tim Pannell **p.13**; Corbis ©Matthew Ashton/AMA **p.14**; Getty Images/Peter Cade **p.9**; Getty Images/Jupiterimages **pp.11**, **12**; Getty Images/Tom Wilson **p.16**; Getty Images/Burke/Triolo Productions **p.19**; Heinemann-Raintree **p.10**; istockphoto ©Leo Blanchette **p.22**; Photolibrary/Blend Images **p.5**; Photolibrary/Monica Jones/Superstock **p.8**; Photolibrary/Superstock **p.18**; Photolibrary/Aneal Vohra **pp.20**, **23**; Photolibrary/Creatas **p.21**; Shutterstock/Christopher Futcher **p.15**.

Cover photograph of symbols of Kwanzaa reproduced with permission of Photolibrary/Corbis RF. Back cover photograph reproduced with permission of Photolibrary/Creatas.

Every effort has been made to contact copyright holders of any material reproduced in this book. Any omissions will be rectified in subsequent printings if notice is given to the publisher.

Contents

What Is a Holiday?

A holiday is a special day.
People celebrate holidays.

Kwanzaa is a holiday. Kwanzaa begins in December.

The Story of Kwanzaa

Kwanzaa honors African history.

Dr. Maulana Karenga started Kwanzaa in 1966. He wanted a holiday to help people come together.

The Seven Ideas of Kwanzaa

During Kwanzaa, people think about seven important ideas.

The first idea is called Umoja.
It stands for unity, or togetherness.

9

The second idea is called Kujichagulia.
It stands for self-determination, or

standing up for yourself.

The third idea is called Ujima. It stands for responsibility and looking out for one another.

The fourth idea is called Ujamaa.
It stands for cooperation, or

working together.

The fifth idea is called Nia. It stands for working hard to help the community.

The sixth idea is called Kuumba.
It stands for creativity.

The seventh idea is called Imani.
It stands for believing in one another.

Celebrating Kwanzaa

To celebrate Kwanzaa, people place special objects on a table.

Seven candles are put in a
candleholder called a kinara. Each
day a new candle is lit.

People play music together. They eat
a great feast together.

People remember the seven ideas
of Kwanzaa.

Kwanzaa Symbols

The kinara is a symbol of Kwanzaa. It reminds people of African history.

The candles in the kinara are symbols of Kwanzaa. They remind people of the seven ideas of Kwanzaa.

Calendar

Kwanzaa begins on December 26.
It lasts seven days.

Picture Glossary

 **candleholder** an object that holds candles. The candleholder used during Kwanzaa is called a kinara.

Index

Note to Parents and Teachers

Before reading

Explain that every December, many black Americans celebrate a holiday called Kwanzaa. Start exploring the seven ideas of the holiday by choosing one or two and asking the children their overall impressions about these ideas. Can the children think of examples in their own lives that connect with each idea?

After reading

Revisit the seven ideas of Kwanzaa. Have the children pick one of the seven ideas and ask them to draw a picture illustrating the idea. Display the drawings around the room as a reminder of how these ideas can be integrated into daily life.